Double High

A Double High-Resolution Text Generator for the Apple II

by

Robert C. Clardy
&
Alan B. Clark

Produced by:
Brian Wiser & Bill Martens

Apple PugetSound Program Library Exchange

Double High

ISBN: 978-1-387-88697-5

ACKNOWLEDGEMENTS

Double High was created by Robert C. Clardy and Alan B. Clark, and originally published by Synergistic Software in 1987. This new manual was produced in coordination with Robert C. Clardy of Synergistic Software and is released with his permission.

Sirius Fonts (36 Large) by Sirius Software 1982.

Apple with TV art from *Higher Text II* manual originally designed by Anson. Colorized and modified by Brian Wiser.

The Cover and Book were designed by Brian Wiser.

PRODUCTION

Brian Wiser → Cover, Design, Layout, Editing
Bill Martens → Screenshots, Layout, Disk Updates

DISCLAIMER

About the Authors

Robert C. Clardy

Robert C. Clardy has been a computer game developer and programmer for home desktop computers and video game machines during the entire lifespan that those devices have existed – over 20 years from the late 1970s through the 1990s and beyond. His experiences encompass birth pains, growth pains, triumphs, failures of the industry, and the many businesses that sprang up and thrived or died during those years.

In early childhood, Robert developed a habit of regular change, always pursuing some new experience or adventure while leaving the familiar behind. This habit encouraged a lifelong fondness for adventures, whether those are in books, movies, games, or software. More importantly, it also encouraged adventures with new business models as well as committing to new computers and industries which did not exist even a short time before.

In 1979, Robert quit his stable and secure-career job with Boeing Aerospace, founded Synergistic Software, and devoted his life to writing software for the Apple II as well as other new home desktop computers as they appeared. Robert wrote adventure games first, but later, the search for change encouraged him to also write utility, business, and educational software.

Robert learned about, programmed, and produced software for many desktop computers and video game machines, as they were released and had their brief time in the sun. Synergistic's computer software development included systems such as the Apple II, Apple IIGS, Atari 800, Atari ST, Commodore VIC-20, Commodore 64, Commodore Amiga, Macintosh, and the IBM PC, along with video game systems such as the Super Nintendo and Sega Genesis.

Synergistic Software was well-known for their variety of games, including: *Dungeon Campaign, Wilderness Campaign, Bolo, Crisis Mountain, Odyssey: The Compleat Apventure, Apventure to Atlantis, Microbe*, and many others.

Beyond Synergistic's own published games, Robert adapted, produced, and programmed noteworthy computer titles published by other companies such as: *Aargh, New York Warriors, Sidewinder, Thexder, War In Middle Earth, Spirit of Excalibur, Conan: The Cimmerian*, and many others. Memorable arcade game adaptations include: *Donkey Kong Jr., Jungle Hunt, Pole Position*, and *Pitstop II.*

Robert's years running Synergistic Software spanned the birth, growth, and total explosion of an industry that had not even existed before that time. Companies and industry giants came and went during the 20 years that Synergistic participated in every aspect of the industry, with many of the major business players of the time. He produced software not only for his own company, but also for other major publishers such as Atari, Activision, Blizzard, Electronic Arts, Epyx, Sierra On-Line, Mindscape, Sony Imageworks, Time Warner, and Virgin Games.

In 1997, Robert quit his long time job with Synergistic Software and started new ventures in a virtual office world that was just then becoming practical. Email, Skype, and sharing files online permitted a business that included principles from around the world, working together to produce products that were marketed online to a download-centric audience. Again, this was a new frontier of technology businesses that Robert surfed and enjoyed.

That pursuit of new experiences colored the rest of Robert's life as well, as he sought out personal adventures in the real world. While never the most extreme at anything he tried, Robert has always been comfortable with where he was, what he did, and the sheer exuberance that comes from trying new things and finding he truly loved every minute of it. If there is a motto for his life, it would have to be, "That was fun, what's next?"

Read more about Robert in his autobiography *Cyber Jack: The Adventures of Robert Clardy and Synergistic Software*. A compilation of enhanced Synergistic Software game manuals from 1978-1982 is in the book *Synergistic Software: The Early Games*. Both books are published by A.P.P.L.E..

Alan B. Clark

Alan B. Clark was a programmer who worked for the Boeing Company in Seattle. He was drawn away from there by Christopher P. Anson, creator and owner of the game publisher Ultrasoft. Alan's earliest commercial works created at Ultrasoft are *Mask of the Sun* and *The Serpent's Star*. He also created the programming language and tools that were used for the program.

Alan also worked with Synergistic Software and Sierra On-Line, authoring a number of titles including: *Double High*, *L.A. Law*, *Beverly Hillbillies*, and *Shadowkeep*. He had more than 40 authorship and production credits in various mainstream computer games at the time of his death in April 1999 at age 40. His last work included *Police Quest: SWAT 2* and *King's Quest: Mask of Eternity*, both released in 1998.

About the Producers

Brian Wiser

Brian Wiser is a producer of books, films, games, and events, as well as a long-time consultant, enthusiast and historian of Apple, the Apple II and Macintosh. Steve Wozniak and Steve Jobs, as well as *Creative Computing*, *Nibble*, *InCider*, and *A+* magazines were early influences.

Brian designed, edited, and co-produced dozens of books including: *Nibble Viewpoints: Business Insights From The Computing Revolution*, *Cyber Jack: The Adventures of Robert Clardy and Synergistic Software*, *Synergistic Software: The Early Games*, *The Colossal Computer Cartoon Book: Enhanced Edition*, *All About Applesoft: Enhanced Edition*, *Graphically Speaking: Enhanced Edition*, *What's Where in the Apple: Enhanced Edition*, and *The WOZPAK: Special Edition* – an important Apple II historical book with Steve Wozniak's restored original, technical handwritten notes. Brian is also the author of *The Etch-a-Sketch and Other Fun Programs*.

He passionately preserves and archives all facets of Apple's history, and noteworthy companies such as Beagle Bros and Applied Engineering, featured on AppleArchives.com. His writing, interviews and books are featured on the technology news site CallApple.org and in *Call-A.P.P.L.E.* magazine that he co-produces as an A.P.P.L.E. board member. Brian also co-produced the retro iOS game *Structris*.

In 2005, Brian was cast as an extra in Joss Whedon's movie *Serenity*, leading him to being a producer and director for the documentary film *Done The Impossible: The Fans' Tale of Firefly & Serenity*. He brought some of the *Firefly* cast aboard his Browncoat Cruise and recruited several of the *Firefly* cast to appear in a film for charity. Throughout these experiences, he develops close personal relationships with many actors, authors, and computer industry luminaries. Brian speaks about his adventures to large audiences at conventions around the country.

Bill Martens

Bill Martens is a systems engineer specializing in office infrastructures and has been programming since 1976. The DEC PDP 11/40 with ASR-33 Teletypes and CRT's were his first computing platforms with his first forays in the Apple world coming with the Apple II computer.

Influences in Bill's computing life came from *Byte* magazine, *Creative Computing* magazine, and *Call-A.P.P.L.E.* magazine as well as his mentors Samuel Perkins, Don Williams, Joff Morgan, and Mike Christensen.

Bill is the author of *ApPilot/W1*, *Beyond Quest*, *The Anatomy of an EAMON*, and multiple EAMon adventure games, as well as a co-producer of many books including *What's Where in the Apple: Enhanced Edition*, *The WOZPAK: Special Edition*, *Nibble Viewpoints: Business Insights From The Computing Revolution*, and co-programmer for the iOS version of the retro game *Structris*. He has written many articles which have appeared in user group newsletters and magazines such as *Call-A.P.P.L.E.*.

Bill worked for Apple Pugetsound Program Library Exchange (A.P.P.L.E.) under Val Golding and Dick Hubert as a data manager and programmer in the 1980s, and is the current president of the A.P.P.L.E. user group established in 1978. He reorganized A.P.P.L.E. and restarted *Call-A.P.P.L.E.* magazine in 2002. He is the production editor for the A.P.P.L.E. website CallApple.org, writes science fiction novels in his spare time, and is a retired semi-pro football player.

CONTENTS

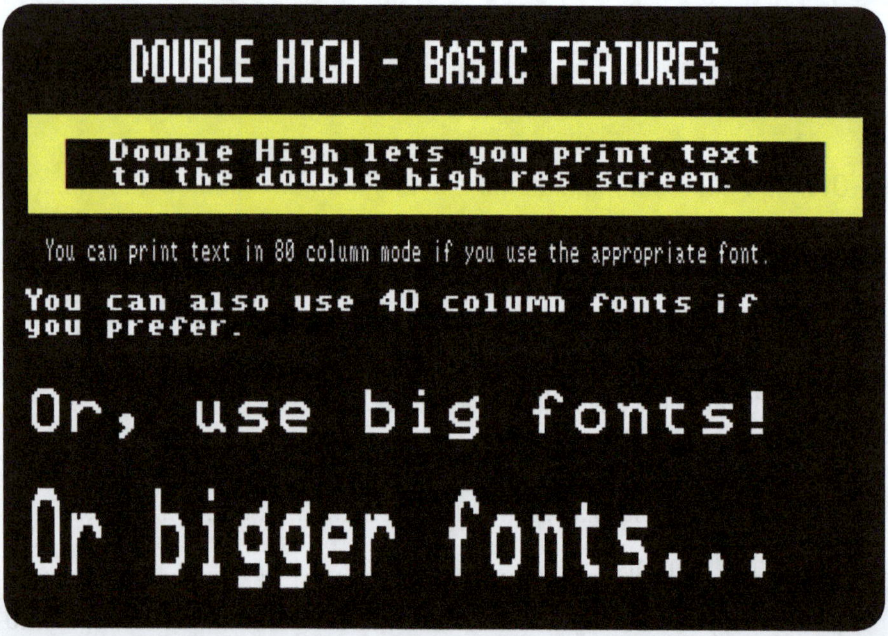
DOUBLE HIGH - BASIC FEATURES
Double High lets you print text to the double high res screen.
You can print text in 80 column mode if you use the appropriate font.
You can also use 40 column fonts if you prefer.
Or, use big fonts!
Or bigger fonts...

Double High is a set of machine language routines designed to let you display text on the Apple II (or Apple compatible's) Double High-resolution graphics screen. You can display text on top of graphs or pictures that you have generated with other programs, or you can use *Double High* by itself to generate your own Double High-Resolution graphics displays. It is particularly easy to create educational programs, demos, games, and productivity programs that would be enhanced with color or graphics, or to just improve the text display capability that the Apple II normally gives you.

Double High was designed to be usable as part of your own programs. You can write your program in BASIC, assembly, "C", or any other language that can directly call a machine language routine. We have made every effort to make *Double High* both powerful and fast and yet easy for any programmer to use. In the pages of this document that follow, we will describe the *Double High* generator itself, how to incorporate it into your own programs, the *Double High* font editor, and how to make your own original fonts.

Ten sample fonts (that you are free to use in your own programs) are included on the disk image, and 36 fonts from Sirius Software's *E-Z Draw* program. You may also, of course, include *Double High* itself on your disks, but if you intend to sell any package that includes

Double High, you no longer need to obtain a license from Synergistic Software, but you should credit Synergistic Software and the new publisher Apple Pugetsound Program Library Exchange (A.P.P.L.E.).

Also on this disk image is a demonstration program that illustrates some of *Double High's* features. Try running the demo from the boot menu that you see when you boot the other side of this disk. If you see anything in the demo that you would like to do in your own programs, just stop the demo (CTRL-RESET is easiest) and list it to your screen or printer. We have made the program very easy to read and understand. There are comments describing what the code is doing at each "page" of the demo. Use the techniques illustrated in the demo to make your program easy to write, easy to edit, and easy to read.

```
DOUBLE HIGH

1. Information about Double High
2. Run the Double High demo
3. Run the Double High font editor

    Select 1, 2, or 3. ■

  by Robert Clardy and Alan Clark
Copyright 1987 Synergistic Software
```

If you have ever used *Higher Text*, another Synergistic Software and Apple Pugetsound Program Library Exchange (A.P.P.L.E.) product, you will find much in *Double High* that is familiar. All of the Higher Text features are included in *Double High* except screen scrolling. This one feature was dropped since it was somewhat slow on the Double High-Res screen and was of little use to most *Higher Text* users.

2

In addition to *Higher Text's* basic features, *Double High* adds a number of useful additional capabilities. If you have worked extensively with *Higher Text*, have no fears. You can load your *Higher Text* fonts directly into the *Double High* font editor and save them in Double High-Res form. You can also expand them automatically, loading a *Higher Text* small font as either an 80 column or 40 column font, depending on whether you want maximum characters per line or text that is easier to read on color monitors.

Double High is provided on a DOS 3.3 disk. This is because DOS 3.3 users cannot easily convert anything supplied on a ProDOS disk into DOS.

ProDOS users, however, can convert DOS 3.3 disks to ProDOS very easily with the *Filer* program from Apple Computer or with various copy programs such as *Copy II Plus*. All of the *Double High* programs, routines, and fonts work equally well in ProDOS as they do in DOS.

To make a ProDOS version of *Double High*, first use your disk utility program to format a blank disk with ProDOS. Then, copy PRODOS to the disk. Then, copy BASIC.SYSTEM to the disk. Then, copy all of the *Double High* files to the disk (yes, they will all fit). Finally, rename the HELLO program to STARTUP. You're done! Label your new disk appropriately and file away your original copy in case you ever need it again.

DOUBLE HIGH - PRINT STYLES

Double High gives you a number of options on how your text should appear on the screen besides the variations in font size and proportional printing.

For instance, you can have **BOLDFACE** words in your text for extra emphasis. Or, use *ITALICS* or INVERSED text if that is more appropriate.

You can also use UNDERLINED words or TALL text.

For even more variety or emphasis, you can *MIX AND MATCH MODES AT WILL!*

DOUBLE HIGH - TEXT POSITIONING

Double High lets you place text on the screen in a mode that automatically emulates the Apple's text screen. It also lets you place text anywhere on the screen that you want.

You can have superscripts[1] or subscripts[2].

Put your text anywhere you want it!

Horizontally too!

PROGRAMMING WITH DOUBLE HIGH

Double High should work on any Apple II or Apple look-alike that has a Double High-Resolution screen. It has been specifically tested on the Apple IIe, the enhanced Apple IIc, the Apple IIc, the Apple IIGS, and the Laser 128. The program cannot work on Apple II's or Apple look-alikes that do not support Double High-Res such as the Apple II, the Apple II Plus, or the Franklin 1000/1200.

To use *Double High* in your own programs, we first must talk briefly about memory usage. Apple II memory is divided into two 64K banks referred to respectively as Main RAM and Aux RAM. BASIC programs are generally confined to Main RAM. Unfortunately, Main RAM must also play host to numerous other bits of code and data such as DOS (or ProDOS), text page memory, graphic screen memory, various buffers used by the system (keyboard buffer and stack, for instance), etc.

The parts of memory that are available for easy use by the programmer are memory locations $800 (2048) through $9600 (38400). In the middle of this, we have the Double High-Res screen from $2000 (8192) to $4000 (16384). *Double High* itself resides between $800 and $1000 (2048-4096). The fonts used by *Double High* can be placed anywhere in memory. Since the area after *Double High* and before the Double High-Resolution screen memory is somewhat short for most programs ($1000 - $2000 or 4096 bytes), it is generally recommended that you put your fonts there and put the program itself after the screen memory.

How do you do that? Assembly language programmers should simply assemble their programs to begin at $4000 or later in memory. Load *Double High* at $800 and load your fonts at any page boundary after $1000. You should be aware that *Double High* fonts can become quite large and you must load them at locations that are big enough to hold them without overlapping something else (e.g. do not load a font that is seven pages long at $1A00. It will overlap the screen).

What about BASIC programs? Normally, the Apple II wants a BASIC program to begin at location $800 (2048), right where we have *Double High* sitting. To put a BASIC program somewhere else, the easiest method is to have a loader program that changes the pointer that the Apple II uses to find its BASIC programs. The start of program pointer is located at location 103 (low byte) and 104 (high byte). To change this from its default value of $800, simply POKE them to some other number before you load your program (see the example below). One other thing that is necessary for this to work is that the first location used by any BASIC program must be a zero. You will also have to POKE that before you load your program.

For instance, assuming that you want your BASIC program to begin in memory immediately after the Double High-Res screen, your loader program should POKE location 104 with the number 64 since your program is to start at location $4000. The high byte is $40 or decimal 64. You must then POKE location $4000 (16384) with a zero and run your real program. A sample greeting program is illustrated below. Be sure to include the run command in the same line of BASIC code that does the POKEs since your Apple II will lose track of where this loader program is in memory as soon as you do the POKEs. This won't matter unless you actually end a line of code at which time your Apple will go looking for the next line. It can't find it (because of the POKEs we just did) and it will get hopelessly lost.

Example Loader Program:

```
10 POKE 104,64: POKE 16384,0: PRINT CHR$(4)"RUN
   PROGRAM": END
```

If you make this the boot program on your disk and if PROGRAM (or whatever name you want) is your actual demo/game/etc. program that will use *Double High*, PROGRAM will be properly located after the Double High-Res screen and you will have no memory conflicts with the screen or with the *Double High* code itself.

Now that you have your program exactly where you want it, what do you have to do next to use *Double High*? The next step is to load *Double High* into memory, initialize it, load a font, and begin printing text to the Double High-Res screen. To load and initialize *Double High*, just BRUN it or BLOAD it and do a CALL 2048 when you are ready to work on the Double High-Res screen.

Before you actually print anything, you must load a font and tell *Double High* where it is. The default font location is at $1000 (4096). If you load a font there, you can begin printing immediately. If you load a font elsewhere, you will need to tell *Double High* where it is by POKEing locations 3 (low byte) and 4 (high byte) with the address that the font is located at. If you load a font at location x, for instance, you would POKE location 3 with x - 256 * INT (x/256) and POKE 4 with INT (x/256). The code example below will get *Double High* loaded and initialized, load an 80 column font at $1000 and print "80 columns" and load a 40 column font at $1400 and print "40 columns" using the appropriate font for each printing. As you can see, you do not need to do anything tricky about the printing itself. Just use the same commands that you would use when working on the text screen and they will properly work with *Double High*.

Example Program:

```
10  D$ = CHR$(4): PRINT D$"BRUN DOUBLE HIGH":
    PRINTD$"BLOAD NORMAL.80,A$1000": PRINT D$"BLOAD
    NORMAL.40,A$1400"

20  PRINT "80 COLUMNS":PRINT:POKE 4,20: PRINT "40
    COLUMNS": END
```

Double High fonts can be any size you want. A normal, average sized font that looks appropriate for 80 column displays requires $361

7

(865) bytes. An average 40 column font requires $652 (1618) bytes. Larger, tall 40 column fonts (such as the COUNTDOWN.T40 font on your disk) require $C42 (3138) bytes. Really large 20 column fonts require $1822 (6178) bytes. The area under the Double High-Res screen contains $1000 (4096) bytes. There is room there for a tall font and an 80 column font, four 80 column fonts, or two 40 column fonts. There is not room for the really large fonts that are on your disk (any font ending with .20). If you want to use one of the large fonts, it too will have to locate above the screen (say at $4000), so your BASIC program must go even higher in memory. You could put your program at $5900, for instance by POKEing 104 with 89 and POKEing 22784 with zero before running your application.

You can have any number of fonts in memory at a time and switch between them at will, mixing font styles and sizes on the same screen. Take a look at the demo program to see this in action. It uses four fonts that are all in memory at the same time.

Once you have initialized *Double High*, your "text" screen will be replaced by the Double High-Res screen. If for any reason you need to return to an actual text screen, you will need to deactivate *Double High* and redisplay the text screen. You can do this as illustrated in the following line of code:

Example: Turning Off *Double High*

```
1000  TEXT: CALL 49920: CALL 1002: REM YOU ARE NOW IN
      TEXT MODE
```

OR

```
1000  TEXT: PRINT D$"PR#0": REM YOU ARE NOW IN TEXT
      MODE
```

To get back into *Double High* without wiping your previous Double High-Res screen, just do a CALL 2051. Your previous display is intact, *Double High* is reactivated and you are looking at the Double High-Res screen.

FEATURES AND COMMANDS

So far, we have only discussed the ways that *Double High* can display text just like on the Apple II's text screen. While there are many uses for this, *Double High* can do much, much more. *Double High* lets you mix your standard text with boldface, italics, underlined text, colored text, extra tall text, different sizes of fonts, and with different styles of fonts. You can also print your text in standard text screen character positions or in a proportional text display mode that is more attractive.

The proportional display mode is the same as is used in the Macintosh display or the text format used in most book/newspaper/magazine publishing. Finally, you can put your text on the screen, combining it with whatever was already there in three different display modes. All of these features are illustrated briefly in the demo program. The paragraphs that follow will discuss each feature briefly and tell you how to get it in your own programs.

Almost all of the *Double High* features are enabled by printing a control character command code that is a mnemonic for the command itself. For instance, if you want to switch to boldface printing, you just print a Control-B character (for bold). To get italics, print Control-I. To turn off any display mode, just issue the same command again (Control-I to turn italics back off after you are through with it). Or, you can just print a Control -N at any time (for normal) to return to the default state of printing simple text with no embellishments.

The code example below illustrates this use of control commands to get *Double High* features. It is recommended that you use string equivalents of the control commands that you want to use rather than simply typing control characters directly in the middle of your print statements. While that will work, it makes your programs difficult to read and edit.

Example of Control Commands:

(assumes *Double High* is running and with a font in place)

```
10  B$ = CHR$(2): I$ = CHR$(9): N$ = CHR$(14): REM
    SETUP A SERIES OF STRING VARIABLES WITH THE
    CONTROL COMMANDS YOU WILL NEED

20  PRINT "This is a test of "B$"BOLDFACE"B$" text
    as well as ";I$;"ITALICS";I$;". You can even
    ";B$;I$;"USE BOTH!";N$
```

This example will print a line of text with boldface text in it, italic text, and boldface and italics at the same time. You can mix and match any of the *Double High* features at the same time to get whatever effect you wish. The example also shows that having semicolons between the string variables (B$ or I$) and the text surrounded by quotes is completely optional. You do need to have the semicolons between strings of commands, however (the B$;I$;). Finally, it shows that you can turn off features one at a time by issuing the same command again or you can turn them all off at once by using the Control-N command.

In addition to the boldface and italics commands, you can also use any or all of the following commands:

CTRL-E   EXCLUSIVE-OR Mode

This feature makes all subsequently printed text be exclusive ored to
the screen, which means that rather than white characters just placed
on top of whatever was already on the screen, the character to be
printed will reverse the colors of whatever was on the screen at that
location. Take a look at the demo for an example of this difficult to
explain concept. You will probably need to experiment with colors
and backgrounds to see what this mode can do for you under different
circumstances. One common application is to use it to print black text
on a colored background. Use the same color for your text as you use
for the background.

CTRL-L   Clear Screen and HOME Cursor

This feature will clear the current text window to whatever color has
been selected with the background color command described below.
As with the normal text screen and BASIC's home command, you
can setup a "window" by POKEing locations 32,33,34, and 35 with
window left (0-79), window width (no more than 80 - window left),
window top (0 to 23), and window bottom (1 - 23 but always greater
than window top). Appendix J of your Applesoft manual discusses
windows in more detail.

CTRL-P   Proportional Text

Displays all subsequently printed text in proportional mode.
Characters are closer together in most cases. The I character takes
up much less space, for instance while the M is actually wider. For
the most part, you can print many more characters per line while in
proportional mode.

CTRL-S   Store Mode

Prints subsequent text to the screen, completely erasing whatever was
at that location previously. This is needed if you want your text to
really stand out or if you want to print over other text that was at that

location on the screen. The default display mode places text into the current screen, leaving the background intact. That mode lets you print on colored backgrounds without leaving a black box around your characters. Try both modes before you decide which is right for any given application.

CTRL-T   Tall Text

Displays all subsequently printed text as double tall characters using the current font.

CTRL-V   VTAB Command

This will move your *Double High* cursor to whatever text screen location has been specified last by Applesoft's HTAB and/or VTAB commands. If you want text in the center of the screen, for instance, you would do VTAB 11: HTAB 40: PRINT V$;"TEXT" where V$ has been defined as the control-V character. If you do not use the control-V command, *Double High* will ignore the Apple's HTAB and VTAB commands. This is to allow the placement of text anywhere on the screen that odd sized fonts require. From assembly language, just use whatever routines you have used before to place a text cursor and print the Control-V before you print text.

CTRL-Y   Underlined Text

Control-U is already used by the right arrow key and we want that to work as it always has.

Several of the commands above refer to the use of colors with *Double High*. You can assign foreground (text) color and background color to any of the Apple's 16 possible colors using the user function from BASIC (from assembly, load the accumulator with the desired color number and JSR to $806). To set the text color to dark blue, for instance, you would put A = USR (1) in your program. To set the background color to dark blue, you would use A = USR (17). The variable A has no significance. The values to use for various colors:

```
 0 = Black text          16 = Black background
 1 = Dark blue text      17 = Dark blue background
 2 = Dark green text     18 = Dark green background
 3 = Medium blue text    19 = Medium blue background
 4 = Brown text          20 = Brown background
 5 = Grey text           21 = Grey background
 6 = Green text          22 = Green background
 7 = Light green text    23 = Light green background
 8 = Red text            24 = Red background
 9 = Purple text         25 = Purple background
10 = Grey2 text          26 = Grey2 background
11 = Light blue text     27 = Light blue background
12 = Orange text         28 = Orange background
13 = Pink text           29 = Pink background
14 = Yellow text         30 = Yellow background
15 = White text          31 = White background
```

When *Double High* first starts, you will have black background and white text selected. You can change these at will, but remember that some colors don't look good together on the Apple's Double High-Res display. Generally, light colored text on dark backgrounds and vice versa work best. To actually use colored backgrounds, you must first select that background color using the USR command, then clear the screen (or current text window) to that color using the clear screen command (Control-L).

The only remaining feature of *Double High* that we haven't mentioned is how to load and save Double High-Res screens. This is something of a problem since the screen is half in Main RAM where you can easily get at it and half in AUX RAM where you cannot. If you have your own routines for loading such screens, use them, but if you do not, *Double High* does have provisions for getting the screen all into Main RAM where DOS or ProDOS can save it. First the procedure, then the problem.

To save a screen, first do a CALL 2057, then BSAVE <name> , A$2000, L$4000 or BSAVE <name> , A8192, L16384 where you replace <name> with the actual name you wish to call the screen. Similarly, to load a screen, you should BLOAD <name> then do a CALL 2060 and it will be moved into the area of memory used for the Double High-Res screen.

The problem with this is that it requires use of the space between $4000 and $6000 for the AUX RAM half of the screen. This is where you may have placed your program or large fonts. If you wish to use this method of loading and saving screens, you must move your program and/or large fonts even later in memory. This method is used by some of the other Double High-Res utility packages such as *Dazzle Draw* from Broderbund, however, so if you wish to load screens made with *Dazzle Draw*, you must use this method.

If you don't care about any other programs, however, you can use an alternative method of loading and saving screens. You can first save the Main RAM half of the screen (BSAVE <name.1> , A$2000, L$2000 or BSAVE <name.1>, A8192, L8192), then do a CALL 2063 which will swap the Main and Aux RAM portions of the Double High-Res screen. Then, simply BSAVE the second half of the screen (BSAVE <name.2>, A$2000, L$2000 or BSAVE <name.2>, A8192, L8192). Then, do another CALL 2063 to swap everything back the way it was.

Whenever you use either of these routines for loading/saving screens, your view screen will look decidedly odd during the load/ save itself since parts of it have been moved. To avoid seeing this odd display (and to make certain that the moves work correctly in all cases), you should turn off double high during the load/save. Do a PR#3 first (as illustrated in the example below), do the load/save, then do a CALL 2051 to re-enter *Double High* with your screens restored. The program sample below saves SCREEN1 and loads and displays SCREEN2.

Example Screen: SAVE and LOAD

```
1000  PRINT D$"BSAVE SCREEN1.1,A$2000,L$2000":
      PRINT D$"PR#3": CALL 2063: PRINT D$ "BSAVE
      SCREEN1.2,A$2000,L$2000": CALL 2063: CALL 2051:
      REM  THE SCREEN HAS BEEN SAVED AND THE DISPLAY
      HAS BEEN RESTORED TO ITS FORMER STATE

1010  PRINT D$"PR#3": PRINT D$"BLOAD SCREEN2.2": CALL
      2063: PRINT D$"BLOAD SCREEN2.1": CALL 2051: REM
      ALL IS NOW LOADED AND WE HAVE DISPLAYED THE NEW
      SCREEN.
```

DOUBLE HIGH - WINDOWS

Double High fully supports the use
of windows. You can setup windows
of any size, shape, or color and print
your text within them.

Print within
any window you
wish.

Print within
any window you
wish.

Print within
any window you
wish.

DOUBLE HIGH - PRINT MODES

Double High has 3 different printing
modes that allow you to get different
effects in your displays. *COMBINE* mode
preserves the background, *STORE* mode
overwrites it and *EXOR* mode reverses
it.

COMBINE	STORE	EXOR

SAMPLE SAMPLE SAMPLE

SAMPLE SAMPLE SAMPLE

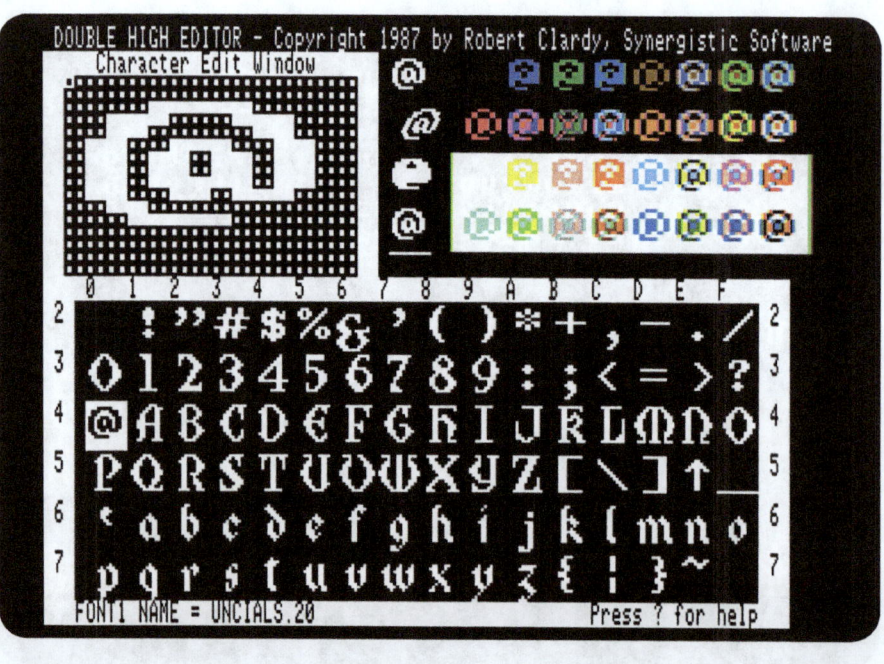

16

The *Double High* font editor lets you create and save your own special purpose fonts. You can load and change any of our existing fonts, directly load any *Higher Text* small or large fonts, or create new fonts from scratch. You can also easily convert any existing font into a proportional font. Once you save your new font, it can be loaded into your own applications as easily as any font supplied with this disk.

When you run the font editor, the screen will clear and you will see an entire font displayed in the bottom 2/3 of the screen. If you want to browse through fonts to see how they look (and to which keys odd characters have been assigned), this is the place to do it. You can load fonts by pressing "L" (for load a font). You will then be asked whether you wish to load a "standard font", a *Higher Text* small font, or a *Higher Text* large font.

The *Double High* font editor will directly load any *Higher Text* font. If you do not have any *Higher Text* fonts, always select "standard font" since all of the fonts provided with *Double High* and on the *Double High* font disks are of this type and require no conversion upon loading as the *Higher Text* fonts do. If you do load a *Higher Text* font, you will also have the option of loading it "single or double wide". Loading a *Higher Text* small font "single wide" will produce an 80-column font while loading it "double wide" will produce a fatter,

40-column font that may look better in color or on color monitors. Loading a large font "single wide" will produce a tall, 40-column font while loading it "double wide" will produce a 20-column font.

When you first run the editor, you will see the NORMAL.P40 font displayed. The naming conventions that we use will give you some idea of the size and style of the font. You are free to follow our conventions or use your own. The *Double High* generator does not care what your font is called.

Font Naming Conventions

Basically, if a font will let you print text that is the size of the Apple's standard 80 column text, we will follow its name with the suffix ".80". If the font is the same size as the Apple's 40 column fonts, the suffix will be ".40". If you can only print 20 characters across the screen (really large fonts like *Higher Text's* large fonts were), we will use ".20". If a font is taller than normal, we will use the letter "T" in the suffix. ".T40", for instance, is a double tall, 40 column font. Most of *Higher Text's* large fonts can be automatically converted to this form.

Finally, if a font has been altered to look its best in proportional printing mode, we will add the letter "P" to the suffix as in the proportional font "NORMAL.P40". The number used does not indicate how many characters will actually fit on a line of the screen, but a rough approximation of the font size itself. Proportional fonts, for instance, can cram much more text on a line than a non-proportional font of the same size.

Character Editing

Back to using the font editor. In addition to the font itself, you will see the character edit window. You will use this window to actually alter individual characters in the font.

Movement Controls

To edit a character, use the I, J, K, and M keys to move a cursor around the font to select the character you wish to edit. Then press the "P" key to pull the character into the edit window. In the edit window, use the W, A, S, and Z keys to move the edit window cursor around.

Editing Controls

Press the "X" key to set a bit in the character or the "C" key to clear a bit. You can also press the Open Apple key with either the "X" or "C" keys to turn on set mode or clear mode respectively. As you move the edit window cursor, you will automatically set or clear every bit you pass over. Press the "X" or "C" key by itself to turn off set or clear mode.

You can also use the control W, A, S, or Z keys to scroll the entire contents of the edit window in the appropriate direction (as those keys are laid out on the keyboard). Finally, when the character is satisfactory, just press RETURN to return it to the font.

19

You can use this feature to rearrange your font as well as changing the characters. Move the font cursor on top of some character, pull it into the edit window, move the font cursor to some other character position and press RETURN.

The character that you lifted will then be placed at the new location in the font. Of course, it is still at the other location as well. While you are editing a character, you can press "V" to view all versions (bold, italic, underlined, and colored) of the character you are working on. You can also press "B" to change the background color that the colored characters are displayed against.

In addition to moving characters around within a given font, you can also easily move characters between fonts. The *Double High* font editor lets you load two separate fonts at the same time. Press "F" to display the alternate font at any time. You can pull a character from one font, press "F" to switch fonts, then RETURN it to the second font. This lets you mix and match characters from many different fonts if you need to.

Loading and Saving

To save a font, press "O" for output. You will be prompted for a font name and whichever font is currently displayed will be saved with that name. To load a font, press "L" for load. You will be prompted for whether you wish to load a standard font (any font produced by the Double High editor, including all the fonts on all of the *Double High* font disks) or a *Higher Text* small font or a *Higher Text* large font. If you do not have access to *Higher Text* fonts, just forget these options. If you do have *Higher Text* fonts, you can load them directly into *Double High*. They will automatically be converted into Double High-Res format.

Using Higher Text Fonts

You also have the option of doubling any *Higher Text* font that you load. Loading a small font without doubling will result in an 80 column font. Doubling it gives you a 40 column font that looks better in color. Loading a large font gives you a tall 40 column *Double High* font. Doubling a large font gives you a 20 column *Double High* font.

In addition to getting font data from our provided fonts and from *Higher Text* fonts, you can also grab any character sized graphic image from any Double High-Resolution screen such as a *Dazzle Draw* screen. Press "G" for grab. You will be prompted for a screen name (or given the option to use the screen already in memory if there is one).

The screen will load and be displayed with a large cursor showing. Move the cursor around with the I, J, K, and M keys (as if you were moving the font cursor around) and press "P" to pull in whatever is under the cursor. That data will be pulled into the font edit window and may be returned to either of the fonts you are currently working with.

Working With Fonts

While you will probably usually be working with existing fonts or modifying some current font, there may be times when you will want to start a new font completely from scratch. This requires a brief discussion of how *Double High* fonts are formatted. A font includes a table that specifies how many bits tall the tallest character in the font is as well as the width in bytes (7 bits or dots per byte) of each character. To make an entirely new font, you will have to build this table.

For this purpose, you can use the "N" command (for new font). When you press "N", you will be prompted that the current font that you are looking at is about to be wiped from memory. Be sure that you have saved any work that you have done to it before continuing. If you continue with your new font, the current font will be cleared and you will be prompted for the total height of your new font and the width of an average character such as the "B" or "H" character. *Double High's* current fonts are:

FONT TYPE	HEIGHT	AVERAGE WIDTH
80 Column	8 bits	1 byte
40 Column	8 bits	2 bytes
40 Column Tall	16 bits	2 bytes
20 Column	16 bits	4 bytes

Decide what you need and answer the prompts appropriately. In estimating a font's height, remember the average number of bits tall of capital letters plus the number of bits you wish to allow for descenders (that part of a lower case letter that goes "below the line") such as is required for the lower case "q", "g", or "p". The *Double High* 80-column font uses 7 bits for capitals and 1 bit for descenders. Apple's text font also uses 7 tall and 1 bit descender. Of course, you can elect any height you wish. Don't feel constrained by what others have done in the past.

One other command not yet described is the "E" command to switch to the other editor. This will take you to a bitmap editor that is described in the next section of this document. As with the multiple fonts, you can take a character between the two editors by pulling it into the edit window, switching editors and returning it to the font in the other editor.

Finally, when you are through editing fonts, just press "Q" to quit to BASIC. You can reenter the editor with everything intact by typing "GOTO 1000" and pressing RETURN.

DOUBLE HIGH - PROPORTIONAL PRINTING

You can use Double High to print in a mode that emulates the Apple's standard text screen display.

Or, you can print with the more sophisticated look of the proportional printing mode to get the look used on the MacIntosh or in professional publications!

Proportional Fonts

To make a font look its best when you print it in proportional mode, you should left justify each character within the character edit window. Pull each character into the window, use the control-A (scroll left) command to move it against the left edge of the edit window and press RETURN. It also improves the font's look to minimize serifs, the small lines that appear at the top or bottom of many letters, essentially for decorative reasons.

Non-Proportional Fonts

Non-proportional fonts should have each character centered within its "size". For instance, 80-column fonts generally allow 7 bits for each character. You should center each character within those 7 bits. A 40-column font should be centered within a 14 bit wide window.

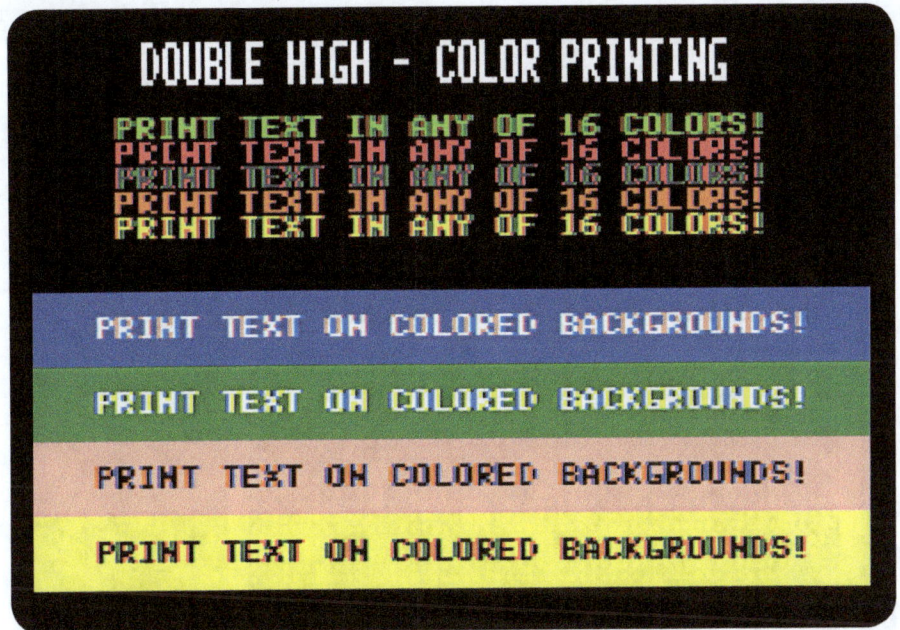

Color Fonts

To make a font look its best when displayed in color, all vertical lines should be at least 4 bits wide, preferably more.

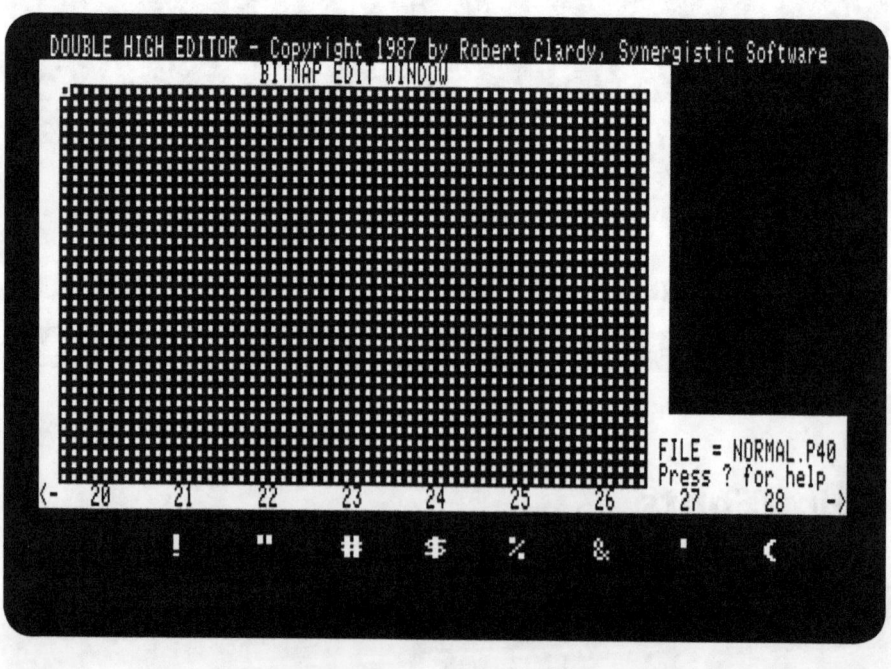

BITMAP EDITOR

Double High is fast enough and versatile enough (you can put a "character" of any size anywhere on the screen) to be used for easily displaying or animating large animated images instead of character data. The bitmap editor was intended to help you design and edit this type of data. You can also use it, of course, to make huge fonts if you wish. Basically, it has all the same features as the character editor except it has a much larger edit window and it only displays part of the "font" at a time.

The edit window will accommodate images 56 bits wide and 32 bits tall. If you need to make even larger images, just use two or more "character" positions to make a single large figure. When you pull a character into the edit window, it will also appear to the right of the window in its normal size. You can move this copy around using the arrow keys, then pull another character into the edit window. Its image also appears to the right of the edit window, not erasing the previous image. Move the second image around until it is placed above or beside the previous one to see how they will look together.

This editor and display mode were used in the *Aliens* game sold by Activision, so you can see that impressive, commercial quality animation effects can be achieved using the *Double High* bitmap editor.

25

All of the commands described in the section on the Font Editor apply to the Bitmap Editor as well. Press "?" to see a summary of the commands if you can't remember them all.

FONTS

Nine fonts are included with *Double High* that represent different sizes: 20-column, 40-column, and 80 column, along with Tall and Proportional versions.

Apple.20

```
■ ! " # $ % & ' ( ) * + , - . /
0 1 2 3 4 5 6 7 8 9 : ; < = > ?
@ A B C D E F G H I J K L M N O
P Q R S T U V W X Y Z [ \ ] ↑ _
` a b c d e f g h i j k l m n o
p q r s t u v w x y z { | } ~
```

Countdown.20

```
■ ! " # $ % & ' ( ) * + , - . /
0 1 2 3 4 5 6 7 8 9 : ; < = > ?
@ A B C D E F G H I J K L M N O
P Q R S T U V W X Y Z [ \ ] ↑ _
` a b c d e f g h i j k l m n o
p q r s t u v w x y z { | } ~
```

Countdown.T40

```
  ! " # $ % & ' [ ] * + , - . /
0 1 2 3 4 5 6 7 8 9 : ; < = > ?
@ A B C D E F G H I J K L M N O
P Q R S T U V W X Y Z [ \ ] ↑ _
` a b c d e f g h i j k l m n o
p q r s t u v w x y z { | } ~
```

Normal.20

```
  ! " # $ % & ' ( ) * + , - . /
0 1 2 3 4 5 6 7 8 9 : ; < = > ?
@ A B C D E F G H I J K L M N O
P Q R S T U V W X Y Z [ \ ] ↑ _
` a b c d e f g h i j k l m n o
p q r s t u v w x y z { | } ~
```

Normal.40

```
  ! " # $ % & ' ( ) * + , - . /
0 1 2 3 4 5 6 7 8 9 : ; < = > ?
@ A B C D E F G H I J K L M N O
P Q R S T U V W X Y Z [ \ ] ^ _
` a b c d e f g h i j k l m n o
p q r s t u v w x y z T ¦ M ~
```

Normal.P40

```
  ! " # $ % & ' ( ) * + , - . /
0 1 2 3 4 5 6 7 8 9 : ; < = > ?
@ A B C D E F G H I J K L M N O
P Q R S T U V W X Y Z [ \ ] ^ _
` a b c d e f g h i j k l m n o
p q r s t u v w x y z T ¦ M ~
```

Normal.P80

```
■ ! " # $ % & ' ( ) * + , - . /
0 1 2 3 4 5 6 7 8 9 : ; < = > ?
@ A B C D E F G H I J K L M N O
P Q R S T U V W X Y Z [ \ ] ^ _
` a b c d e f g h i j k l m n o
p q r s t u v w x y z { | } ~
```

Old.English.20

```
■ ! " £ $ 4 & ' [ ] * + , - . /
0 1 2 3 4 5 6 7 8 9 : ; < = > ?
@ A B C D E F G H I J K L M N O
P Q R S T U V W X Y Z [ \ ] ↑ _
' a b c d e f g h i j k l m n o
p q r s t u v w x y z { | } ~
```

Roman.20

```
■ ! " # $ % & ' ( ) * + , - . /
0 1 2 3 4 5 6 7 8 9 : ; < = > ?
@ A B C D E F G H I J K L M N O
P Q R S T U V W X Y Z [ \ ] ↑ _
' a b c d e f g h i j k l m n o
p q r s t u v w x y z { | } ~
```

Uncials.20

```
■ ! " # $ % & ' ( ) * + , - . /
0 1 2 3 4 5 6 7 8 9 : ; < = > ?
@ A B C D E F G H I J K L M N O
P Q R S T U V W X Y Z [ \ ] ↑ _
' a b c d e f g h i j k l m n o
p q r s t u v w x y z { | } ~
```

Sirius Fonts are part of Sirius Software's *E-Z Draw* program. All 36 of these fonts can be used in both *Higher Text Plus* and *Double High*. In *Double High*, they can be viewed in two modes: Large Font Single width (S) and Large Font Double width (D):

Astra S

Astra D

Boldtype S

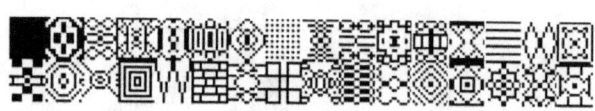

Boldtype D

Border S

Border D

BorderLetters S

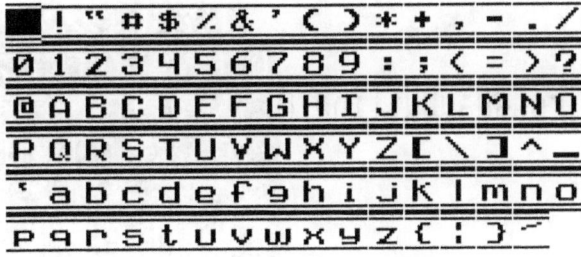

BorderLetters D

Broadway S

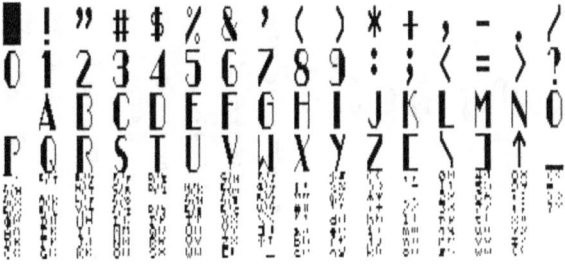

Broadway D

BroadwayOutline :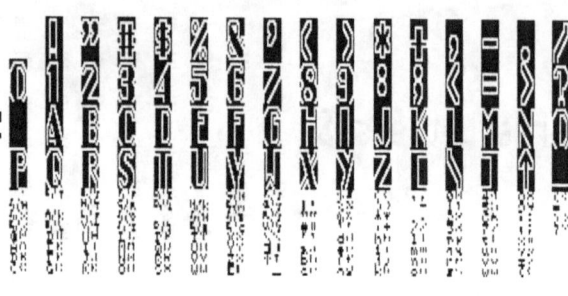

BroadwayOutline I

CoopOutline S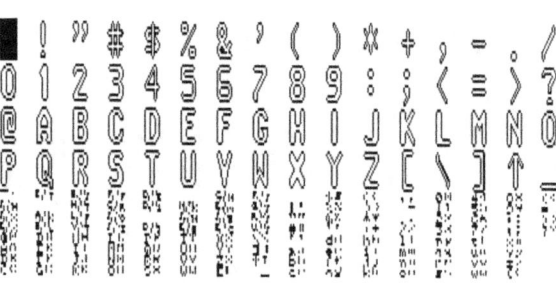

CoopOutline D

Countdown S

```
  ! " # $ % & ' [ ] * + , - . /
0 1 2 3 4 5 6 7 8 9 : ; < = > ?
@ A B C D E F G H I J K L M N O
P Q R S T U V W X Y Z [ \ ] ↑ _
` a b c d e f g h i j k l m n o
p q r s t u v w x y z { | } ~
```

Countdown D

```
  ! " # $ % & ' [ ] * + , - . /
0 1 2 3 4 5 6 7 8 9 : ; < = > ?
@ A B C D E F G H I J K L M N O
P Q R S T U V W X Y Z [ \ ] ↑ _
` a b c d e f g h i j k l m n o
p q r s t u v w x y z { | } ~
```

Cyber S

```
  ! " # $ % & ' ( ) * + , - . /
0 1 2 3 4 5 6 7 8 9 : ; < = > ?
@ A B C D E F G H I J K L M N O
P Q R S T U V W X Y Z [ \ ] ↑ _
@ a b c d e f g h i j k l m n o
p q r s t u v w x y z
```

Cyber D

```
  ! " # $ % & ' ( ) * + , - . /
0 1 2 3 4 5 6 7 8 9 : ; < = > ?
@ A B C D E F G H I J K L M N O
P Q R S T U V W X Y Z [ \ ] ↑ _
@ a b c d e f g h i j k l m n o
p q r s t u v w x y z
```

Expanded S

```
  ! " # $ % & ' ( ) * + , - . /
0 1 2 3 4 5 6 7 8 9 : ; < = > ?
@ A B C D E F G H I J K L M N O
P Q R S T U V W X Y Z [ \ ] ↑ _
` a b c d e f g h i j k l m n o
p q r s t u v w x y z { | } ~
```

Expanded D

```
  ! " # $ % & ' ( ) * + , - . /
0 1 2 3 4 5 6 7 8 9 : ; < = > ?
@ A B C D E F G H I J K L M N O
P Q R S T U V W X Y Z [ \ ] ↑ _
` a b c d e f g h i j k l m n o
p q r s t u v w x y z { | } ~
```

Frankfurter S

```
  ! " # $ % & ' ( ) * + , - . /
0 1 2 3 4 5 6 7 8 9 : ; < = > ?
@ A B C D E F G H I J K L M N O
P Q R S T U V W X Y Z [ \ ] ↑ _
```

Frankfurter D

```
  ! " # $ % & ' ( ) * + , - . /
0 1 2 3 4 5 6 7 8 9 : ; < = > ?
@ A B C D E F G H I J K L M N O
P Q R S T U V W X Y Z [ \ ] ↑ _
```

Ninety's S

```
  ! " # $ % & ' ( ) * + , - . /
0 1 2 3 4 5 6 7 8 9 : ; < = > ?
@ A B C D E F G H I J K L M N O
P Q R S T U V W X Y Z [ \ ] ↑ _
  a b c d e f g h i j k l m n o
p q r s t u v w x y z { | } ~
```

Ninety's D

```
  ! " # $ % & ' ( ) * + , - . /
0 1 2 3 4 5 6 7 8 9 : ; < = > ?
@ A B C D E F G H I J K L M N O
P Q R S T U V W X Y Z [ \ ] ↑ _
  a b c d e f g h i j k l m n o
p q r s t u v w x y z { | } ~
```

Old_English S

```
  ! " £ $ & ' [ ] * + , - . /
0 1 2 3 4 5 6 7 8 9 : ; < = > ?
@ A B C D E F G H I J K L M N O
P Q R S T U V W X Y Z [ \ ] ↑ _
  a b c d e f g h i j k l m n o
p q r s t u v w x y z { | } ~
```

Old_English D

```
  ! " £ $ & ' [ ] * + , - . /
0 1 2 3 4 5 6 7 8 9 : ; < = > ?
@ A B C D E F G H I J K L M N O
P Q R S T U V W X Y Z [ \ ] ↑ _
  a b c d e f g h i j k l m n o
p q r s t u v w x y z { | } ~
```

Pinball S

```
  ! " # $ % & ' ( ) * + , - . /
0 1 2 3 4 5 6 7 8 9 : ; < = > ?
@ A B C D E F G H I J K L M N O
P Q R S T U V W X Y Z [ \ ] ↑ _
` a b c d e f g h i j k l m n o
p q r s t u v w x y z
```

Pinball D

```
  ! " # $ % & ' ( ) * + , - . /
0 1 2 3 4 5 6 7 8 9 : ; < = > ?
@ A B C D E F G H I J K L M N O
P Q R S T U V W X Y Z [ \ ] ↑ _
` a b c d e f g h i j k l m n o
p q r s t u v w x y z
```

Roman S

```
  ! " # $ % & ' ( ) * + , - . /
0 1 2 3 4 5 6 7 8 9 : ; < = > ?
@ A B C D E F G H I J K L M N O
P Q R S T U V W X Y Z [ \ ] ↑ _
` a b c d e f g h i j k l m n o
p q r s t u v w x y z { ¦ } ~
```

Roman D

```
  ! " # $ % & ' ( ) * + , - . /
0 1 2 3 4 5 6 7 8 9 : ; < = > ?
@ A B C D E F G H I J K L M N O
P Q R S T U V W X Y Z [ \ ] ↑ _
` a b c d e f g h i j k l m n o
p q r s t u v w x y z { ¦ } ~
```

Script S

```
  ! " # $ % & ' ( ) * + , - . /
0 1 2 3 4 5 6 7 8 9 : ; < = > ?
  a b c d e f g h i j k l m n o
p q r s t u v w x y z [ \ ] ↑ _
  a b c d e f g h i j k l m n o
p q r s t u v w x y z
```

Script D

```
  ! " # $ % & ' ( ) * + , - . /
0 1 2 3 4 5 6 7 8 9 : ; < = > ?
  a b c d e f g h i j k l m n o
p q r s t u v w x y z [ \ ] ↑ _
  a b c d e f g h i j k l m n o
p q r s t u v w x y z
```

Slope S

```
  ! " # $ % & ' ( ) * + , - . /
  1 2 3 4 5 6 7 8 9 : ; < = > ?
@ A B C D E F G H I J K L M N O
P Q R S T U V W X Y Z [ \ ] ↑ _
  A B C D E F G H I J K L M N O
P Q R S T U V W X Y Z
```

Slope D

```
  ! " # $ % & ' ( ) * + , - . /
  1 2 3 4 5 6 7 8 9 : ; < = > ?
@ A B C D E F G H I J K L M N O
P Q R S T U V W X Y Z [ \ ] ↑ _
  A B C D E F G H I J K L M N O
P Q R S T U V W X Y Z
```

Typewriter S

```
█ ! " # $ % & ' ( ) * + , - . /
0 1 2 3 4 5 6 7 8 9 : ; < = > ?
A B C D E F G H I J K L M N O
P Q R S T U V W X Y Z [ \ ] ↑ _
a b c d e f g h i j k l m n o
p q r s t u v w x y z
```

Typewriter D

```
█ ! " # $ % & ' ( ) * + , - . /
0 1 2 3 4 5 6 7 8 9 : ; < = > ?
A B C D E F G H I J K L M N O
P Q R S T U V W X Y Z [ \ ] ↑ _
a b c d e f g h i j k l m n o
p q r s t u v w x y z
```

OTHER FONTS

The nine fonts provided with *Double High* as well as *Higher Text Plus* fonts, *Wickerwork Fonts*, *Sirius Fonts*, and any other fonts created with either *Higher Text Plus* or *Double High* will work with the *Double High* package. Any programs written to use the fonts can also use the fonts and effects.

Please consider purchasing A.P.P.L.E.'s *Higher Text Plus* manual, which is another wonderful font-editing tool, and has printed samples of over 90 compatible fonts.

We expect that a number of you will be creating new fonts for use with *Double High*. If you don't mind sharing your fonts with others, we encourage you to send us a copy for inclusion on future font disks. When submitting a font, please let us know if you want credit for your work. By sending a font to Apple Pugetsound Program Library Exchange (A.P.P.L.E.), you are agreeing that it may be included in some future font disk without any payment, license, or agreement. Let's get a lot of fonts together for all of us to use!

For historical interest, two additional disks of fonts of various sizes and styles were planned, but never released by Synergistic Software according to Robert C. Clardy:

FONT DISK 1: Foreign Languages

Various sizes of fonts for general European languages (includes Germanic, Spanish, and Scandinavian characters), Russian, Greek, Hebrew, Katakana, Hiragana, Punic, and Arabic (somewhat incomplete because of the limitations of the Apple keyboard).

FONT DISK 2: Fancy Fonts

Various sizes of a wide variety of ornamental English language fonts such as Broadway, Block fonts, Shadow fonts, etc.

Font Editor

?	Display the Help Screen
I, J, K, M	Move cursor around the font characters
P	Pull Character into Window
N	New Font
F	Display Alternate font
L	Load a font
O	Save a font Out
G	Grab any character from Double Hi-Res screen
D	Disk Catalog
E	Switch to the other editor
Q	Quit to BASIC
GOTO 1000	Re-enter the editor

Edit Window

W, A, S, Z	Move edit window cursor around
X	Set a bit in window
OA-X	Turn on Set Bit Mode
C	Clear a bit
⌘-C	Turn on Clear Bit Mode

V	View all versions of character
B	Change background color
<Return>	Put edit window into selected Font placement
Arrows	Move Bitmap around View Window

File Names

.20	20 Characters Across
.40	40 Characters Across
.80	80 Characters Across
.T	Tall
.P	Proportional

GLOSSARY

Definitions used in this glossary may often refer to terminology within the context of, or pertaining only to the characteristics of, the *Double High* program, and not necessarily to general usage.

ACCESS – To locate and retrieve data.

ADDRESS – Memory location, usually expressed in hex.

ALGORITHM – A sequence of steps which may be performed by a program or other process, which will produce a given result.

ALLOCATE – To set aside or reserve space.

ALPHABETIC CHARACTER – Any one of the letters A through Z (uppercase and lowercase).

ALPHANUMERIC – Consisting of letters, numbers, and other symbols such as punctuation marks and mathematical symbols.

APPLE – (1) The round fleshy fruit of a Rosaceous tree (Pyrus Malus). (2) A brand of personal computer. (3) Apple Computer, Inc. manufacturer of home computers.

APPLESOFT BASIC – A floating-point BASIC interpreter that is included in ROM. It was the successor to Integer BASIC. See *BASIC*.

ARGUMENT – The value on which a function operates.

ARITHMETIC OPERATOR – An operator, such as +, that combines numeric values to produce a numeric result.

ARRAY – Matrix of variable data. This data is accessed by programs to fulfill a need for table style data in an easy to manage format.

ASCII (American Standard Code for Information Interchange) – A character encoding standard that translates uppercase and lowercase letters and symbolic characters into a 7-bit binary representation having the values 0 to 127. The eighth bit, parity and framing bits are not part of this definition.

ASSEMBLER – A program used to translate as assembly language program into the machine language used by a processor.

ASSEMBLY LANGUAGE – A language similar in structure to machine language, but made up of "mnemonics" and "symbols" that are converted to the machine language of a processor by the assembler. Well-written assembly language programs usually run faster and use less memory than BASIC programs, but they usually take longer to write and longer to test and debug than BASIC programs.

BACKGROUND – In *Higher Text*, the field upon which characters are printed, also used as a color reference by the Ctrl-B function.

BASE – In number systems, the exponent at which the number system repeats itself; the number of symbols required by that number system.

BASIC (Beginner's All-purpose Symbolic Instruction Code) – A programming language that is designed to be easy to learn and use, and encourage people to use computers for simple problem-solving operations. Originally developed at Dartmouth College.

BINARY – The base 2 number system, composed solely of the numbers 0 and 1.

BINARY FILES – Binary files save machine language programs, binary data (which might be automatically gathered from sensors and generated by analog-to-digital converters), etc. Such material may be of arbitrary length and may include in its body any possible binary combination of bits.

BIT – Abbreviation for "Binary DigIT." Either of the binary digits 0 or 1. See *Byte*.

BLOAD – Binary program load.

BLOCK – Storage methodology used by ProDOS for placing data on a floppy disk. Under ProDOS, a 140K 5.25" floppy disk holds 280 blocks (0~279) of 512 bytes each.

BOOT – The process of starting a computer system ("booting up"). A cold boot is starting the computer after it was off. The operating system (DOS 3.3 or ProDOS) is loaded into memory. A warm boot is a reloading of the operating system without a power-down sequence.

BRANCH – To resume program execution at a new location. GOTO and JMP (jump) are branch instructions.

BRUN – Binary program run. The BRUN command in DOS 3.3 and ProDOS causes a binary program to be loaded into memory and run.

BSAVE – Binary program save. The BSAVE command in DOS 3.3 and ProDOS causes the binary data in some portion of memory to be saved as a disk file.

BUFFER – Large temporary memory storage area.

BUG – A program error, often called "an undocumented feature."

BYTE – The amount of storage required to represent one character. Hexadecimal or Decimal representation of eight binary bits: 0~255 in Decimal, $00~$FF in Hexidecimal. 8 bits = 1 byte. 1,024 bytes = 1K or Kilobyte.

CALL – Executes a machine language subroutine contained within the called memory location and onward. Continues until the program code contains an RTS.

CARRIAGE RETURN – The key used as an end of line or end of input terminator. Also called the RETURN key.

CATALOG – A list of all files stored on a disk, sometimes called a "directory."

CHARACTER – A single byte, letter, digit, or other symbol.

CHIP – Tiny pieces of silicon or germanium containing many integrated circuits that perform specific tasks for a computer.

CHR$(x) – Applesoft function which prints the alphanumeric or special character specified by the ASCII value assigned to x.

CLEAR – In the *Higher Text* editor, removes a dot from the matrix.

CODE – (1) A number or symbol used to represent some piece of information in a compact or easily processed form. (2) The statements or instructions that make up a program.

COMMAND – An instruction to the program, usually input by the user.

COMPILER – A program which translates a high-level language into the machine code used by a computer.

COMPLEMENT – In colors, the opposite; the color 180° opposed in a color wheel. Blue and orange are complementary colors.

CONCATENATE – To join together, making one character string from two, as in C$ = A$ + B$.

CONDITIONAL BRANCH – A branch that depends on the truth of a condition or the value of an expression.

CONFIGURATION – A specific group of software or hardware in a standard format.

CONSTANT – A symbol in a program representing a fixed, unchanging value. Compare to "Variable."

CONTROL CHARACTER – A special character created by simultaneously typing the "Control" key and another alpha character. These keys are used in the editor for cursor movement, text formatting, and other specified functions. Control-G can be shown as ^G.

CPU – Central Processing Unit. See *Microprocessor*.

CTRL – The "Control" key.

CURSOR – (1) A marker or symbol that delineates where the next action will take place. (2) A programmer who can't find the reason a program is crashing.

DASH (-) – Command that runs a BASIC, machine, EXEC, or interpreter program in ProDOS only.

DATA – Facts or information used by or in a computer program.

DEBUGGING – The process of detecting and correcting errors in a computer program.

DECIMAL – The base 10 number system, composed of the numbers 0 through 9, inclusive.

DECREMENT – Decrease value in calculated steps.

DEFAULT – Nominal value or condition assigned to a parameter when not otherwise specified by the user.

DELETE – Command that removes a file from its directory.

DELIMITER – Symbol to separate data fields.

DIRECTORY – List of files on diskette or part of a group of files on a hard drive. In ProDOS, each directory has a name rather than the "Slot x, Drive x, Volume x" designation in DOS 3.3.

DISKETTE – A 5.25" or 3.5" disk. Apple II 5.25" floppy disks typically hold 140K, and 3.5" disks typically hold 800K of data.

DISPLAY – The output of the Apple II or program to a television set or monitor.

DITHERING – A process of dot mixing to produce additional hi-res colors.

DOS – Disk Operating System such as DOS 3.3 or ProDOS. The user interface between a computer and the applications program. An OS allows the user to execute programs and perform disk operations.

DOT MATRIX – A grid or graph of specific dimensions used for drawing a character by placement of certain dots.

DUMMY – Data with no significance, "GET A$" is a dummy if used just to halt a program.

EDITOR – Text-editing program that allows text to be entered into a data file and manipulated as desired.

ENTER – A means to obtain access to a program or subroutine from keyboard or direct mode.

ERROR MESSAGE – Message that notifies the user of an error or problem in the execution of a task or program.

EXEC File – A DOS text file which, when called by the EXEC command, reads data into Apple II memory as if it were entered from the keyboard.

EXECUTE – Perform an action specified by a program or computer operator.

EXIT – A means to return to BASIC or direct mode from within a program.

EXPRESSION – A formula in a program describing a calculation to be performed.

FAC – Floating Point Accumulator.

FID – A file transfer utility on the Apple DOS 3.3 master diskette.

FIELD – Contains data which would not normally subdivide.

FILE – Data that has been saved to a diskette, such as a BASIC program or a word processing document.

FILENAME – Name of a file that has been saved to diskette.

FIRMWARE – Those components of a computer system consisting of programs stored permanently in read-only memory. Cards for printers and other devices contain firmware.

FLAG – A data bit used to indicate the state of a device or the result of an operation.

FONT – A specific *Higher Text* character set.

FORMAT – Prepare a blank diskette to receive and store information by dividing its surface into tracks and sectors.

FP (FLOATING POINT) – Floating Point BASIC as included in Applesoft.

GENERATOR – *Higher Text* operating system that includes at least one font.

HEX – Abbreviation of hexadecimal, the base 16 number system.

HEXADECIMAL – The base 16 number system, composed of the numbers 0 through 9, and A through F. Usually notated with a '$' prefix. Hexadecimal is a useful shorthand for describing the contents of a byte, with each hex digit describing half of a byte.

HEX DUMP – Formatted listing of hex data.

HIGH ORDER – The byte containing the value of the left most two digits of a hex expression.

HI-RES – High-Resolution graphics.

HOME – The normal or default position of a cursor.

IMBED – To implant or place within.

IMMEDIATE MODE – The normal condition of an Apple II when a program is not running and commands may be entered from the keyboard.

INCREMENT – Increase value in calculated steps.

INITIALIZE – (1) To set to an initial state or value in preparation for some computation. (2) To prepare a blank disk to receive information by dividing its surface into tracks and sectors.

INPUT – (1) Information transferred into a computer from an external source, such as a keyboard, disk drive, or modem. (2) The act or process of transferring such information.

INSERT – In editing, to place additional characters within a string or to add dots to a matrix.

INTEGER – Number without fractional parts in the range -32768 to +32767.

INTEGER BASIC – The BASIC interpreter for the first Apple II. Succeeded by Applesoft BASIC.

INTERPRETER – A program which translates instructions written in a high level to machine code as the program is executed.

INTERRUPT – (1) To temporarily stop a process. (2) A signal created by either hardware or software to demand the immediate attention of a machine's CPU, there by stopping execution of any code that is being executed by said CPU. (3) In data communications, to take an action at a receiving computer that causes the ending computer to end a transmission.

INVERSE – The opposite of, usually applying to the Inverse Mode in text fonts or numbers.

I/O (Input/Output) – The transfer of information in and out of a computer. Used frequently in connection with peripheral devices.

IRQ – Interrupt requests.

JUMP – Another term for a branch.

KILOBYTE (K or KB) – Used with numbers to denote "kilo" or one thousand. 1K = 1,024 bytes. 64K is 64 times 1,024 bytes, or 65,536 bytes.

LABEL – Symbolic name for an address, often expressed in mnemonic form.

LINE – One line of text on the display screen. In Text Mode, 23 lines are available.

LINEFEED – Moves the cursor on the screen down one line. The ASCII character is Control-J.

LOAD – Command that brings a BASIC program into memory from a file.

LOADER – Program that calls up machine code from mass storage and loads it into memory for execution.

LOCK – Command that protects a file from being accidentally renamed, deleted, or altered.

LOGICAL OPERATOR – An operator, such as AND, that combines logical values to produce a logical result.

LOOP – Section of a program that is executed repeatedly until some condition is met such as an index variable reaching a specified ending value.

LOW ORDER – The byte containing the value of the right most two digits of a hex expression.

LO-RES – Low-Resolution graphics.

L.S.B. – The Less Significant Byte of the two-byte pair.

LSB – Least Significant Bit.

MACHINE LANGUAGE – Data groups which are interpreted as instructions to be executed by the processor. See *Assembly Language*.

MEMORY – See *RAM (Random Access Memory)*.

MEMORY LOCATION – A unit of main memory that is identified by an address and can hold a single item of information of a fixed size. In the Apple II, a memory location holds one byte, or 8 bits of information.

MENU – A screen display allowing the user to select from a number of options.

MICROPROCESSOR – A computer processor contained in a single integrated circuit, such as the Apple II's 6502 or 65C02 microprocessor.

MNEMONIC – Symbolic abbreviation containing characters helpful in remember an application or function, such as an assembly language instruction.

MOD – Algorithm which returns the remainder of a division operation (must be simulated in Applesoft BASIC).

MODE – A particular sub-type of operation.

MODULE – A portion of a program devoted to a specific function.

MONITOR – (1) A closed-circuit television receiver. (2) A program which allows you to use your computer at a very low level, often with the values and addresses of individual memory locations. Monitor commands are used to communicate with the Monitor.

M.S.B. – The More Significant Byte of the two-byte pair.

MSB – Most Significant Bit.

NIBBLE (or Nybble) – (1) A 4-bit unit of data, or half a byte. (2) One of the best and longest-running magazines for the Apple II and Mac, created by entrepreneur and business expert Mike Harvey. (3) "What are we going to call this series of bits? How about a bite, but spell it with a 'y'! So what do we call half a byte? A 'nybble', obviously!" (attributed to Werner Buchholz at IBM, circa 1956.)

NULL – Having no value.

NUMERIC – An ASCII character in the 0-9 range.

OBJECT PROGRAM – The program produced by a compiler or interpreter from a high-level program.

OFFSET – Value, often used with or as an index to locate related data and add to a base value.

OPERATOR – A symbol or sequence of characters such as + or AND, specifying an operation to be performed on one or more values (the operands) to produce a result.

OUTPUT – (1) Information transferred from a computer to some external destination, such as the display screen, a disk drive, a printer, or a modem. (2) The act or process of transferring such information.

PAGE – Each page of memory in Apple II computers consist of 256 bytes. That is to say, $00 to $FF would be one page. A 32K machine would have 128 pages, a 48K machine would have 192 pages, while a 64K machine would contain 256 pages of memory. After the Zero Page ($0000~$00FF), each page is described by the first two digits of its 4 digit hexadecimal address.

PARALLEL – A method of data handling in which all the bits composing a word are transmitted simultaneously.

PARAMETER – A constant or value that a program requires to function, often specified by the user.

PARSER – Section of interpreter that formats listing of a BASIC program.

PATH – A specified route to a specific subdirectory used in ProDOS.

PC – Program Counter.

PEEK – BASIC command which returns the decimal value of a specified memory location.

PERIPHERAL – An external device connected to a computer such as a printer, modem, monitor, or disk drive.

POINTER – A register memory location containing the memory address of data or instructions.

POKE – BASIC command which stores a decimal value in a specified memory location.

PR# – Command that sends output to the Apple II slot number specified.

PREFIX – A settable pathname that indicates a directory file.

PROCESSOR – A generic term for that part of computer hardware performing arithmetic and logical operations. See *Microprocessor*.

ProDOS – The major operating system for Apple II computers, that stands for Professional Disk Operating System.

PROGRAM – A sequence of instructions to be followed by the computer to carry out desired operations.

PROGRAM CONTROL – Normally used to refer to instructions issued while a program is running.

PROMPT – To remind or signal the user that some action is expected, typically by displaying a distinctive symbol, a reminder message, or a menu of choices on the display screen.

PROTECT – To prevent an area of memory from being overwritten.

QUIT – Exiting a program and returning to the operating system.

RAM (Random Access Memory) – The volatile, temporary storage area in the computer that requires power to maintain its contents.

RAM DRIVE – The use of RAM to emulate a disk drive for temporary drive storage.

READ – To transfer information into the computer's memory from a source external to the computer (such as a disk drive or modem), or into the computers processor from a source external to the processor (such as a keyboard or main memory).

REGISTER – Single RAM memory or microprocessor storage location, usually for temporary use. A, X, Y-Registers and S, P, PC-Registers.

RELATIONAL OPERATOR – An operator, such as >, that compares numeric values to produce a logical result.

RENAME – Change the name of the file.

RESET – A key, which is part of a combination that causes the computer to re-boot a program. To Stop and warm start the computer.

RESIDES – A specific memory area in which a program or data may be found.

ROM (Read Only Memory) – A memory device from where operating instructions and other programs reside permanently and cannot be altered or added to.

ROUTINE – A program which performs a specified task or function.

RS-232 – A standard voltage interface allowing a serial connection between the computer's communications port and an external device such as a modem or a printer.

RUN – The command to execute a BASIC program.

RWTS – Read-Write Track-Sector. These are the Diskette input and output routines.

SAVE – Command to save the BASIC program currently in memory to a file on disk.

SCROLL – To move a line of text (usually upward) on the screen.

SECTOR – The tracks on Apple 5.25" diskettes are subdivided into sectors. The sector is the smallest unit of information that can be written to, or read from, a diskette at one time. Each sector contains one memory page (256 bytes) of usable information. Each track contains the same number of sectors, so the physical length inches or centimeters of a sector on the outermost track is longer than that of a sector on the innermost track. Sectors on the outermost track and the innermost track take the same amount of time to pass by the read head.

SERIAL – A method of data handling in which the bits composing a word are transmitted one after the other.

SET – In the *Higher Text* editor, to place a dot in the dot matrix.

SLAVE DISKETTE – A disk that has been formatted for a specific system type and will only boot on that system type.

STACK – A section of memory used to hold addresses or data items. The page of 256 memory locations from $0100 to $01FF (decimal 256~511) is called the Apple System Stack, as well as memory Page 1. The Stack is used in conjunction with the S-Register or Stack Pointer to provide positive control of the system in situations where control is passed from one portion of a program to another.

STATEMENT – An instruction line in a high-level language. In BASIC, smallest portion of a program complete in itself. Delimited by a ':' or end of line.

STRING – A group of ASCII characters that are alpha, numeric, punctuation, or control.

SUBROUTINE – A section of frequently used operations in a program which are treated as small separate programs.

SUFFIX – In *Higher Text*, a portion of a command that requires additional preceding data.

SYNTAX – The formal structure of an argument or command.

SYNTAX ERROR – An error which specifies to the user that the structure of the line of BASIC code is improperly formatted or that it is missing a required element such as quotation marks.

SYSTEM – A collection of routines or programs operating as a single entity or program.

TABLE – List of values, words, data, etc. that may be referenced by a program.

TEXT – A line or string of ASCII characters.

TEXT FILE – A file containing an arbitrary string of ASCII characters interspersed with occasional carriage returns to specify the end of a line.

TEXT SCREEN – The normal Apple II screen display, not used by *Higher Text* or other graphical programs.

TOGGLE – To switch from one mode to another. In *Higher Text*, this is usually performed by issuing the same command.

TOKEN – One byte hex representation of a BASIC or other high level language command.

TRACE – A debugging method in which the program is executed one instruction at a time, and sometimes the register contents can be examined after each step.

TRACK – Apple 5.25" diskettes have 35 tracks under DOS 3.3. Each consists of a circular recording path at a fixed distance from the center of the disk. Thus, each is like a very thin, at ring, concentric with all the others. They are numbered from 0 (the outermost track) to 34 (the innermost track).

VAL – Applesoft command that solves the value of a string. Also, the founder of A.P.P.L.E.

VARIABLE – Alphanumeric representation which may assume or be assigned a number of values.

VECTOR – Address to be branched to.

VOLUME – In DOS 3.3 and ProDOS, volume refers to floppy disk and hard drive storage.

VTOC (Volume Table of Contents) – On a 5.25" diskette Sector 0 of Track 17 (the track which is equidistant from the innermost and outermost tracks) is reserved for the VTOC.

WHY – Questions that programmers ask that have no answer.

WINDOW – Portion of screen display blocked off for special use.

WOZ – Steve Wozniak, an Apple Computer Inc. co-founder, inventor of the Apple-1 and Apple II computers, all-around genius, nice guy, über geek, philanthropist, and longtime supporter of the A.P.P.L.E. user group.

WRITE – To transfer information from the computer to a destination external to the computer (such as a disk drive or modem) or from the computers processor (such as main memory).

WWA – *What's Where in the Apple: Enhanced Edition* – a very useful programming reference book, also published by A.P.P.L.E.